SNAPS

snaps

POEMS BY VICTOR HERNANDEZ CRUZ

RANDOM
HOUSE
NEW YORK

This book is for

Diana, Pamella & Paul

who stick like glue

for Joan a teacher who teaches

for Butchy who smokes like a chimney

for Candy for the one hour

& Carmen for the two minutes

SNAPS

HALF A Page from Square Business

It is cold Tuesday.　　gray sky.　　hot tar.　　your misery
working.
　　　　　imagine:
　　　　　　　　glass sticking out of tar.　　wind
　　　　　　　　blowing.　　your daughter dead.
　　　　　　　　all your horror dreams come true,
　　　　　　　　at the same time.
　　　　　　　　your wife felt up by brown wrinkled
　　　　　　　　hands.
it is 12 midnight.　　all this belongs to me & it is
beautiful.
　　　　　but my true nature is gentle
　　　　　& the stare of a mad eye.

First Claims Poem

who i break my head against
who i jump on
who i fall into   who i am

who i am   a skull   eyes looking for trouble
to leave the shapes you got the same i can-
not do that to crush & twist them i will

a skull   eyes   black hair   a final word
a lip opening unusual a third open a
cut the taste of blood a finger kissing
slowly an eye   an open window where i
live   black burlap   malcolm   x hanging on
the wall burning candle the sound of a
high-pitched conga drum Ishmael's book is
still to be read mongo coming out from the
speakers   conga going up walls   there is
still time   there is still hope   there is time
i think to fail again & again&again & again
there is time for all this   there is time for Ish's
book there is time to win a prize there is
time   it is time for those who will win
the awards   i have time & in time i will
fail

who i break my head against
who i jump on
who i fall into   who i am

it is time to deserve

who i deserve
what do i deserve

if i do not deserve anything on this earth
if not a drop of things here is mine

i deserve
i deserve
with all the hand clappings
all the space from here to the moon.

Coming Down

1
closed windows
on all the six floors
everything coming out
big black dog on first floor
one toilet open on the 3rd floor
my floor
my uncle   a strange man
from P.R. kissing a girl
on the last floor   silently
i would watch   no one is
coming i would say

looking for wood
(there was a small fire-
place where we lived
at first later they
took it out)

across the street fat
girls hung out of windows
licking the streets
giggles away   one wore
the same sneakers for
years   in the snow
in the rain
on the hot tar   another
was sandra the oldest
who always had tight skirts
once running up the stairs
she heard a noise.

2
Moe & Carlos
on the top floor
their place always
on fire   a surprise
that we got out that
building alive
we did things like
robbing a car & crashing
it into a building
robbed cigars from a drug
store   &   threw bottles
at the hospital windows.

3
1958
the snow
lexington avenue
going into the train
even cold then
pushing into 96th
street
even cold past that
going past that
past 86th street

huge windows
packages coming back.

4
big basement on the corner
the blue lights
all the girls going in

big huge girls with nice lips
skinny & stupid girls
come down to sweat off make-up
the huge big ones to fall
on the sofa in the back
a skinny one who danced real
close   real close   giving you
all those bones   but giving
you something   another skinny
one was missing a tooth smack
in the front   they say she fell
down stairs   but who knows.

5
outside the buildings are cool
toward third avenue with hands
in pocket smiling at the windows
making it with half eyes
with all the river veins
telling whores apart from the
stupid ones
a wino leaning
walking walking till 116th
up high stairs
a door
music.

6
weds. night
the heavy head
february is my birthday
it was raining & carmen
was sure   more sure than

9

me sometimes   debby was
scared all the time
lucy was big   she took
junk thru her nose
laura liked three guys
at the same time
she had a strong body
carlos knocked off miriam
she took him to her mother
no lights
noise on the stairs
no big thing.

7
carmen was mine
those eyes looking on me
say what
shits coming out your face
stupid puerto rican.

8
everybody had them slick
cons
& the same smile
catching cabs downtown
finally coming
& they say
they won't wear them
shoes any more
the buildings talking to
each other
listening to the radio
lost in wires

in waves   under concrete
in the air   under the glass
under the metal
weds. is the heavy head
sitting here writing
i wonder why it's so
stupid looking from the river.

Back to/Back to

o mondays is o.k./ last monday a building fell
so what
o moving back now   back to
back

i never go back to georgia
i never go back to georgia

packing
man what strange shit you taking
back
man what big shits you pushing

any
how

moving let's go
let's go fast up up up
where
by the candy store   la vieja
la vieja is still alive &
chuchifritos & rice & beans by
la bodega de pepe   by the corner
anti-poverty housing toms
by chelas & the kids yelling & pushing
people down

hey hey
what's happening
que pasa

o new walls
talking loudly

o monday is o.k.
monday is o.k.

PHASE 2/4 HOURS

(SLIT HIS THROAT)
IN THE MARCH AFTERNOON
OF THE STREET OF
LOVE
SLIT HIS THROAT
IN THE BLACK NIGHT
OF LOVE
WITH LOVE FOR MANKIND
THREW HIM IN THE BATH
TUB OF BLOOD
THE PIG
SLIT THE THROAT OF THE PIG
THE BATHTUB FULL OF
CLEANSING BLOOD
THE MAN
KING OF UGLINESS
MONSTER OF LIES
MR. MACHINE
TOOL OF GREASE OF DIRT
IN THE MARCH AFTERNOON
OF FALLING THINGS
A BEAUTIFUL SHOW
OF HEADLESS RATS
SQUEAKING.

A Poem for DOWNTOWN
(some thoughts on a bus ride)

trees on the left
from the right side
trees
miles of trees
till concrete
white walls   hit
your eyes

dead stone
an attack
against the windows
the sun on the glass

two policemen
holding hands
on the corner
behind paper walls
they are holding
hands

(the faggot potential
of america)   the   cops

ah   ah
superman flies by
up ahead
someone stomped
a french puddle
how terrible
but have no fear

that flying he-man
is here   he saved
the day
          & batman & robin
on 86th street
swinging from buildings
to building   what
happen   some punks
robbed   the diamonds
of the grand old lady
of the virgins   last
untouched piece on earth

a cloud floats on top
(i hope they never
catch the punks)
a cloud that started
spitting

the trees behind
concrete

but on the side
the stones are on the
grass & leaves are floating

on the water
everything is floating
now
      maybe even this bus.

& Stuff Like That

it was
a year ago
tricks were
played all over
i got it
two times
ten dollars
i lost
bombs all over
the same cat
won't pull it twice
on the same sucker
unless he was
a pad boy
then they may
pull it on him
a million times
before he got hip
nothing you could do
unless you sight the guy
& cut him

but
the best thing
is to be tight
with the main man
this way
            you get good stuff
            & you'll do the tricks.

Cocaine Galore I

eyes that rolled on the floor/as they played
mary-lou did the drinks / the last supper
head of wines/ someone stepped on the eyes
of color/colors/on the walls from the eyes
the building dropped the floor/mary-lou of
funny walks/ sister of leans/ hurry up with
the drinks/shit/as they played/ the curtain
began to bleed/& the eyes/ the eyes you know/
jingle bells/everyday of new/everyday of things/
everyday   sunshine/ spoons & bags everyday/

the bad smells of the air/come up coney island/
rackets go round & round/shadows of the sun/
moon & moon glow/the moon is in the water/
line of magic rays/rockets of fourth of july/
independence day/another thing/again/again
colors/colors shooting in the night/red & dark
blue/noise of water/heavy coming/ distance
roar of trains/ sandals sunk in the sand/half
ass/half-ass wet/ half-ass wind/breeze/breeze
or what you call it/bad bangs thruout the night/
up away/ your ears with them/

BLAH   SHA   BLAH BALA
kingsize smoke/ out of space/brooklyn bums
pickpocket thru the crowd/big fire of bright
ness brings day/ darkness/darkness/ & the iron
horse/kicking in loudly/ outside/dark/dark life/
the ladies of the boogaloo going by in hands/or
out of hands/in slow steps going by to cabs or
subways/the corners full with wide-eyed zombies
of the strange parts trying to buy a night for
themselves/mary-lou & plate of mofongo/sunday
morning/ sunshine / sitting back eyes closed/

white powder 1

in the dark corners of buildings
where politicians & their gray men
won't be caught dead
                    are the new arms
smacking themselves heads
                 the chinese
eyes/the red spots of the eyes/have
stories/lean back on piss-dried mattress
open up or melt at the corner
                  the nails
run thru the body scratching out need
now run up / smooth
               burn the shit some
more he said/ it ain't ready
                who said when
the city sleeps/pass the last project/
exchange a deck/bars full of secrets/eyes
follow pool balls/almost falling to the
ground
      in the dark corners
      where brothers wait the hours
walking up & down with sweet soda/wiping
sweat/water spilling/
            the trey bags are
so empty/tongues lick the paper/slowly
moving/
       but missing the light
       missing the light
       & there is so much to see
                like
gringos & their gray men laughing.

IS A DEAD MAN

hopeless
useless
the sound makes
me tremble run
for cover   run
till i hear it
no longer   till
the thought of
it spilling is
gone it will
turn me to soft
yellow to talk
like a bird
all these grown
men i must stare
at all these
guilty bodies
waving at me
coming out the
t.v. set   why
they sing in
silence   they
cook in caves
they kiss with
plastic covers
they dance like
shit is coming
out they ass
or like they
all retarded
why don't i

just cut one &
see if they for
real   they for
real lord they
for real you
gots to live with
this   you gots to
talk with this you
gots to play with
this   in your mind
drop it out you
mind shit
stomp the shit
to the air out
your precious head
out your life
it is there
they live
they have books
they have bands
god help us they
have bands   they
have singers   O

they have singers
who knock you into
orbit   around boredom
snag at the moon
forget they exist
forget they talk
forget where you are
if they come to
your door to sing

26

& play noise   then
you bang them people
up   blow them up
snap their necks
eat their brains out
burn their eyes out
knuckles away
knuckles away
send them fags fly-
ing thru air

hopeless
useless
is a dead
dead world
they selling
here.

today is a day of great joy

when they stop poems
in the mail   & clap
their hands & dance to
them
when women become pregnant
by the side of poems
the strongest sounds   making
the river go along

it is a great day

as poems fall down to
movie crowds   in restaurants
in bars

when poems start to
knock down walls   to
choke politicians
when poems scream &
begin to break the air

that is the time of
true poets   that is
the time of greatness

a true poet   aiming
poems   & watching things
fall to the ground

it is a great day.

Street Scene #1

1

man he'll see like all faggots do Jay ain't around & his girl
has gone crazy walking the street maybe even forgot his
name Sunday is a boss day nothing to do so you find something
strange to do

7 MAN THAT'S IT THE AGE YOU CAME TO THE STREET
COOL BUT CHANGED   LIKE OVERNIGHT & BECAME THE
ONE

it is even strange you know fast they went by fast the toilet
a wall a car an old lady on the roof it is raining & her eyes
are bleeding
they went by fast
a man told you get a dollar yeah a whole dollar a girl say-
ing no maybe right but it went by fast
a stoop asses on it cat runs by bleeding from the head
chip in for the taste chip in time flies

IT WAS A CLEAN HALLWAY & SHE WAS DRUNK SO THEY
    DIDN'T CARE
& ALMOST KILLED HER SHE BLED LIKE HELL BUT SHE WANTED IT
SHE YELLED FOR MORE SEVEN GUYS WERE AROUND HER SOME
    IN THE
BACK SOME IN THE FRONT SOME IN THE MOUTH SOME ON
    HER TITS
BUT SHE WANTED IT & IT WAS BEAUTIFUL

work on them now
sweetie pie it was a nice year all the guys stayed around
& not one got busted

& they got over threats like

                    i'm going to bust your head
because they just got high that summer.

2

BOY Just wait there girl
     just stand there
                    GIRL Come on man what do you
                          think i am, some kind
                          of toy
BOY Be cool
     just be cool
                    GIRL Now looka here
                          i'm sick & tired of you
                          you ain't no big thing
                          anyway
BOY Shut up
                    GIRL Good-bye

3

                    it's green
                    i'm telling
                    you man
                    it just
                    looks blue
                    at night
                    light the match
                    you see
                    stupid
                    O.K.

an ounce man
come on we all could get down

an ounce man
five of us crowd around it
we could do nice.

Ladies' Poem

for who
a girl named barba . . .
what is this

ugly   what else
social worker
striving for more   ugliness
in all the payrolls

two summer jobs

possible for something
or else
run away   fly with a storm
hide from the horrible thing

O but one named carmen
what softness
& other things
those eyes   look
     O how

can we make it

anyway

another named judy
in her
sometimes   i think
find something
dancing later

                    she will
        offer food
        FOOD
                yeah
        i cool tho
                    & say just a bit

        ideas
        how can i be with three
        one ugly
        so two
                    HOW

        but what about
        Sugar
        dancing. always worried.
                    of evil around
                    her. as if she lived
                    in the rich side.

        around the block
        Cookie does her best

        (how can i, so many
        but all so fine)

        diana
        likes to read
        & sometimes she understands
        she even
        talks when she makes love

                        i no good

            she why
        I NO GOOD

&
gloria sitting
sometimes by a place she says her uncle at
but
it matters little
the way she acts
around there
(SO MANY
 SO MANY
            SO)

a skinny girl
three blocks up once said
& it came to pass
others
were less scared
& stayed more often
like to dance too

i know who would first
how
    many
lovers can i turn into poems

lovers into poems
holy shit
lovers' poem

emmie or something like that
was bad

i'll kick you up your
puerto rican ass she told me
one time
i went back sort of
& said
o yeah
she said
yeah

one strange name
chique ta
enough of girls' name
how would they read it
even may kill me   maybe

was summer worker in church
wanted to escape
a smile
catholic
you all catholic
i asked
a smile
a funny loving smile
invites everything
she said
the priest said it
to be evil
so.

cash my check
& pick one up
dance
&

dance
walk ride   kiss
my hands floating

then a stupid polish cat
smiles at me like he knew what was happening
i thought i should take him over
but janitors don't carry much money
besides lucy was fun in that hallway

norma was quiet most of the times
walking down the street
she would almost love me sometimes
i think
when i was there   especially

further uptown
fat emily
scares me, her mouth sometimes opens
to unhuman distances
i begged for my life
& her cousin
more in shape
for many things
but has weird beliefs.
she introduced me to yvonne
yvonne with a high school
ring that no one could miss
she would smile into the night
sometimes saw one of my poems

there was two
on 103rd

to see them
without bumping
into each other
i took great pains
to prevent this
including   running
up some stairs to a
little room that leads to the roof
running & reaching where i thought
one of them would be at   instead
a wall

linda was hip to me
like none of them were
& she even scared me one time
when she said she wanted to marry me
just that
she would type for me   she said
she would read & study for me
& she would have done it
sometimes i wonder

older girls are dangerous
one big one
i think sharon
from the projects
once took a good watch
i had stole from this drunk man on the train
& pawned it
told me the next day

baby with all speed
to it   this is

simple
i said to lilly one time
this other girl
& she fly
what can we do   this world
is full of these things
& this girl just stand there holding on
holding on
knowing what would come   but
holding on

finding out two months later
that night
i went to the block
the corner was dark

was that really you
she asked yesterday
a year later
i said maybe
she walked down the street
holding her stomach
which had a baby inside

maybe one i call pammie
to snag me now

how can i be with them all

after the storm
i go into this other storm
all of them again

different people now
one called gloria
we walked on third avenue
& i notice
how different
if it started to rain now
it would be nice

i can talk
how nasty
woman
shit look
you too slow
it's been too long
woman
beans dig it
no rice
some vegetables
milk
now

Snag

1
i thought of you
early morning
my eyes still not open
your eyes leaning against the wall
& the beautymark behind your knee

(but i'm making this up; am i)

the way you threw your arms
into my coat
& yelled it's too big
but did not matter

anyway
it's early morning

2
who are they over there
singing in a corner
beer cans in hands
passing Luchow's
not looking in to see their boss
or to smell the food

early Sunday mornings
i do things like this
or i think of something better.

The Drive

how this car broke down
yelling
we/we
went head first
how you drive that shit, man
lamppost of murder
landscape move around/
ladies & gents/you all
whaO/
head into window of
we/we
heads & legs hanging out of
car/
yelling
&
smash into something like
empire-waldo-historica-
plates of steak to our heads
& screams/
only your head, lady
parts flew/the waiter of speed
crying
we
yelling up & down
laughing/rolling on the floor
out of breath
grabbing golden hamburgers/with
french fries
hey hex where's T
he's getting some ketchup
O all right
the fucking poll began moving
that's how it happened

going uptown to visit miriam

on the train
old ladies playing football
going for empty seats

very funny persons

the train riders
                    are silly people
                    i am a train rider

but no one knows where i am
going to take this train

to take this train
to take this train

the ladies   read popular
paperbacks   because they
are popular   they get off
at 42 to change for the
westside line   or off
59 for the department store

the train pulls in & out
the white walls   darkness   white walls   darkness

ladies looking up   i
wonder where they going
the dentist   pick up

husband pick up wife
pick up kids
pick up ?grass?
to library   to museum
to laundromat   to school

but no one knows where i am
going to take this train

to take this train

to visit miriam
to visit miriam

& to kiss her
on the cheek
& hope i don't
see sonia on the
street

But no one knows where i'm taking
this train
        taking this train
        to visit miriam.

After the Dancing
        For Pamela

we move
to the whispering
after the dancing

do you dare
for all your dreams
for your sometimes stupid head
dug in the air
passing like cars
from one room to another
for what's left in you
after the dancing
do you sometimes wonder
your skin stretching
your head turning
your ass pushing
your arms flying
do you sometimes wonder
if you let go
if the walls move
if the floor cracks
if the ceiling lights up
& you be there
do you sometimes wonder
if the people cheer
if you get busted
for illegal steps
if the judge say
your boogaloo is ammunition
do you sometimes wonder

we move
the whispering
after the dancing.

Their Poem

Pat
China
& Rosa
all walking
down the street
with carriages
the babies
hanging out
they belong
to my friends
who say:

someday we will get married.

their poem continued
what are you looking in that store window   for what are you
looking
        to die with jingle bells   by whores i know from
        lexington ave. who now make it with politicians
        to die   by a christmas tree   all the lights
        on you
        with $110 in the bank   a ring on your fingers
        a shelf with two books . . . dictionary
        to die with this
.you don't want this
instead look how you dance   talk & scream   how you shine
the lipstick   it's ugly   let me tell you   take it off
it's bad for the hallway   leaning against the mailboxes
how much better it could be   the wind falling on your face
drag your ass this way   when your mother would come
& not see us   when you almost giggled

it just ain't right, she said
they broke the windows & put holes in the building
& Elba's son Ray wanted to be a doctor
he deals medicine to get high on now

WE TOOK WILLY HOME   WITH HIS EYES DRAGGING   ON THE STAIRS
he gave Barbara a baby & she left him & married
now has a house in Brooklyn   & Perry Como records
she plays for her guests   she won't come around
because it's too dirty   her husband is stupid
bought a big car   he didn't know them white folks
like little ones   to put liberal magazines on the back seats
they even have pancakes for breakfast

Judy got a secretary job
                    with a lawyer
                            pays good
                                    she likes it
                                    because she carries
                                    a brief case & newspaper

when she goes dancing saturday her bottle of Wilson
sticks out of her pocketbook
maybe i should tell her

Tito standing with me   as we listened to my uncle's
stupid advice he thought he was smart & really
believed what he said

Rosa is not married   her son is now in school
she keeps it up her mother's house when she parties
that big house on the corner   where i got lost
chasing her friends   one time in the dark

room to room   my hands in the air
hoping for better things to touch

she had a fake brother we never saw him
but they say he was in jail

Julio wears forty-two-dollar knits with 'gators
& shining slacks   that were handmade
because he works overtime   & deals cocaine
his girl loves him   they want to get married in the fall
they will wear rings & walk together on third avenue
her stomach falling in front of her   he will offer soda
& run down:
                    do we need milk or something

Carlos with cons   & new blue shades   goes to college
plays pool at the bar on the corner of 109th Street

either i'm stupid or i don't know what you're talking about,
he said
turning to look in the mirror
                                middle-class stupidity staring
                                at him

Chino came back with an army suit on   i guess this was
suppose to be hip
when he walked with his old girl   & took pictures
by the park
he kissed his mother hard &   caught a train back

Carmen
there was three Carmens   this one from the projects
we went to the East River when it rain & stared

at the water   but not for long
Norma came & stay with Harold in the shadow of a tree

Carmen stares at my   clothes   & wonders
why i don't wear knits like all the people
she talks to me now when i visit   though
she thinks i'm a little crazy

Helen is a jewish neighbor   so i told her what the names
meant
we lived on the same block   i explained to her
we went upstate together
we came out together
went dancing together
gave our girls babies together
went on junk together
& didn't get off together

Helen did not understand

(O funny, it used to be babycakes, but not no more funny)

Mildred was big
somehow she got small & skinny   she visits me
sat on me half a day once   telling me lies
& kissing me   showing me the things her boyfriend
buys her   a good leather jacket   & beatnik earrings
a new book   by Dracula or somebody   she smiles
on the train going uptown   i'm sweating bricks

Benny writes to me from jail
he robbed a drugstore & beat a policeman up on
broadway   then he stole a car   & was caught

kissing the tires in Florida

JADE TURNED INTO JIVE DUST   WONDERED IF IT WAS VOODOO
i told him it was panamanian red when he recovered
he lowered his head & continued to ask what happened
Candy was the girl i was to marry
but we ran into storms   & i had to bust her lip
one time
& she didn't speak to me & winter came
i saw her shadow going past me   the last time

Little Man always comes around   with his scars
& his son that runs & walks
Little Man would understand   even now   when i see him

he wonders
why i still carry a knife
them days are over, he tells me & i stare at him
& he understands

maybe that last one was too close to me
she got upset when i put my hand in her blouse
she made coffee for me
&
all these years   how old i must be getting
but no
        i turn to the mirror & stare at my youth
        & wonder at my intelligence.

/ SISTERS /

we eat
chinese food
on broadway
then uptown
to where we thought
but
make a phone call
find out
claudia
mary
pamella
carmen
candy
diana
     bust with us
     to argue
     with gold hunters
seventh avenue line
ernestine
& ida boone
you want to
go see the movies
paul tell carlos
about them bitches
he's been rapping to
tell him
we left school
early
let's go to louie's
house
that's what we did

in the daylight
like that
we heard mongo
& the five-stair steps
something is missing
they said
debby slowly
whispered
& we didn't see
the clock
we saw pictures
in louie's room
a red light
for late at night
to count by or
to see your hand
we turned & laughed
talked
looked out the window
going down the elevator
held hands
letting all the lights
on lexington guide us
we ate
we ate soul
& kissed
& hugged thru
the streets
had an argument
with a building
but flush that
keep it going
honeychild

honeychild
ladies   ladies
do that to us
they all hung
from the windows
take them out
take them to the park

we turned
the corner
dancing
cause we were
going home.

Energy

is
red beans
ray barretto
banging away
steam out the
radio
the five-stair
steps
is mofongo
chuchifrito stand
outside down
the avenue
that long hill
of a block
before the train
is pacheco
playing with
bleeding
blue lips

Cities
(moved singing/ laughing/feeling/
talking/ dancing)

1
subway in
subway out
grove street
nine blocks
fifth ward
downtown
jersey city
the avenue
empty & lit
the store owners
hanging out
the doors
making legal
robberies.

2
we trust
the stairs
of a building
& they are
not even ours.

3
new projects
elevators
highways
snow
pot & hashish

stereo music
pucho & the latin
soul brothers
disturb
anglo-saxon
middle-class
loving
americans.

4
washington st.
the kind of party
you have to take
your hanky out
a bag of smoke
with a nail
inside
i mean/shit
i've seen a whole
lot of shit pass
for grass
but a nail.

5
together
drag your feet
in the snow
it's new year's
they say.

6
the kidney foundation
wants more money

& if you eat cheerios
you'll have power
so says the t.v.
that woke me up.

7
central
dance-hall
musicians
smoke before
they come out
the red exit
sign
the blue lights
girls with
black leather
pants
sweet
talk
&
sweat.

8
little cousins
play on your
fingers & head
& want kisses
before you leave.

9
they had women
in their pockets
a story of the

harbor
clowns came to town
hollering
they kick they ass

shit like that.

latin & soul
   for Joe Bataan

1

some waves
              a wave of now
                            a trombone speaking to you
a piano is trying to break a molecule
is trying to lift the stage into orbit
around the red spotlights

a shadow
the shadows   of dancers
dancers   they are dancing   falling
out that space   made for dancing

they should dance
on the tables   they should
dance inside of their drinks
they should dance on the
ceiling they should dance/dance

thru universes
leaning-moving
              we are traveling

where are we going
if we only knew

with this rhythm   with
this banging   with   fire
with this   all   this   O
my god i wonder   where are

we going
      sink into a room full of laughter
      full of happiness   full of life
      those dancers
      the dancers
            are clapping their hands
            stomping their feet

hold back them tears
            all those sentimental stories
cooked uptown   if you can   hold it for after

we are going
      away-away-away
      beyond these wooden tables
      beyond these red lights
      beyond these rugs & paper
      walls   beyond   way past
      i mean way past them clouds
      over the buildings   over the
      rivers   over towns   over cities
      like on rails   but faster   like
      a train   but smoother
      away past stars
      bursting with drums.

   2
a sudden misunderstanding
            a cloud
            full of grayness
a body thru a store window
            a hand reaching
            into the back

                              pocket
a scream
          a piano is talking to you
          thru all this
          why don't you answer it.

Free Spirit
    for Ray Barretto

marching in space/summer streets/windows
upward/sunshine
loose   loose   it was you
                            it was you

hanging
coming at me
with your drums/you
soul drummer   you who went
away   away   but came back & coming
so much energy   doing what you want
what you want most   marching in space
all over the earth   a snake
a good spirit   a new head

summer streets/listen   ohohoh
he's already at that point
red hot oh
he's alrighty there   listen
now
listen now

sha
sha
sha

where am i
shooting stars/again windows
again
again fire

71

again scream
again come
marching in space
in space
do it all
listen
finger   finger   wha
                                wha

go to the river
go where you want to

explosion
explosion

watch ray   watch ray
good & strong   moving moving
moving
now
& forever   moving like the
earth

moving like rain/summer streets
summer
your fingers bleeding
bleeding   your eyes closed
eyes closed   bleedy conga
listen
listen
hear.hear.hear.   everything
everything

the bronx is ours   the bronx

take the bronx & shhhhhit
listen
the dance   the dance
O the stairs   O the windows
will be broken   O so many hearts
dancing   so many legs swinging   so
many heads shaking   O so many people
living O so many loving
listen

sha sha sha sha

O so many dancing
O so many dancing
shooting their hearts
shooting stories
shooting

now
now
again them windows
again them windows
breaking

here we go

soul drummer

sleep   sleep   sleep
down   down   down
softly
the piano plays our memories
our dreams   our loves   the

piano player he is wondering
listen, he's looking at you
he's talking
& ray & ray is screaming
screaming
is screaming

soul
soul drummer

you marching in space
you talking   you
flying

you already there
nothing stopping you
you are magic
magic
magic
espiritu libre
espiritu libre

everywhere   everywhere
the song   the moves   the
moves
you are back
you are back

blood
your eyes were closed
you are back

sha sha

& no lines
but what comes   now
now like the indians
O marching in space

espiritu
libre
espiritu libre/

descarga en cueros

louie was dragging his legs on the floor
at the bar people's drinks flew out they hands
the vibrations knocked people to the floor/& the
lights began to bust/& the floor to crack
it started raining sweat & drinks/people on top
of tables/or coming out of all kinds of holes/the sound
engineer went home/a wall fell down & the place opened
up to the street/people ran & whistled/ & laughed
almost choking themselves/daisy put her ears in her
pockets/carlos' head was leaning against a wall/sally
was crying & yelling O my god/the floor began to rock
people fell off the balcony/t.p. was smiling/his face
ready to rip/o.k. you win/hands in the air ready to
fly/heads outside beyond the buildings.

the education

the second floor
belongs to larry
hanging from the
light bulbs
insulting
respectable educators
likewise the bathroom
is his

(better not open the
  door & let all that
  smoke get out)

moving between doors
& bells
& small dark rooms
where you could smoke
or snort garbage cans
full of coke

(only a paid fool
  would say this didn't
  happen)

three days/out of Franklin

the soul is a beautiful thing
& i live by the soul
when i walk
it takes me
               today
i didn't go to school
i read
got high
ate
read
wrote
got high
spoke to carlos
saw the indians
on t.v.
& in my mind
& heart
they kick
the white man
in the ass
went down
got high
took a bus
honeychild
& claudia
giggled
about paul
homemade
chicken
& rice
found a dime

sticking
in the tar
jefferson park
the wind
talks
night
morning
no school
black coffee
corn muffin
read david's
felix
listened
to joe bataan
wrote
i learned
today
beautiful
soul
went down
spoke to some
children
& slowly
remembered

chino
singing
baby
O
baby
in the
hallway
at 12-17

i smiled
at the rain
when it fell
from the window
wrote
head
night
morning
no school
but the world
& my soul
& all the love
that wants to
blow up
like joe bataan's
trombones
night

three days
with myself
& the world
soul is beautiful
thing
the smell of
everything
ahead
the earth
& all the people/

                        victor hernandez cruz
                        exiled from franklin
                        december 14 to 19

BORN TO BE BURNED

1
it was no dream
it kissed you
& you flew away
with your head
on fire.

2
the same radio
plays
two years
fifteen times to the
floor
clothes
& wood

&
t.v.s
&
beds
&
baby carriages
&
chairs
&
the river
on the
picture
on the
wall.

3

it was slow spring
just coming by
no dream
screams
easter screams
asking god to come
his head
first hit the
garbage can
it fell hard
from the sixth floor
it bounced
& smashed into
the tar
he did not move
the god he called
did not come
thru the flames/

For Tiny

If Tiny.
if Tiny said, no shit looka de moon
how it turn green & shits
But i faster
bending corners
Now
     lipping & stuff
some rice after
no beans today
Talk people to death
innocent bystanders dead
If Tiny
feeds her lungs smoke
that will turn yellow
funny feelings in the head
Flipping in blue sneakers
Right there
If Tiny
carries one pencil in her notebook

do the bounce
they crazy anyway
shingaling
they crazy anyway
in the street
all night long
the crazy bounce
the people's bounce
they crazy anyway
the boogaloo
the fuck is this

this is the dance
blessed by the lord
it tears your ass
& if you had some smoke
you move like flash
the people do it all night long
they crazy anyway

If Tiny
shines like gold
& moves like storms
& brings down walls
(i help her out
 i scream in halls
 i smoke all day
 the man gets scared
 he thinks we loud
 that is the truth
 we boss & hip & cool
 we crazy anyway)

How You Feel

the rats took over
the store downstairs
eddie called & said
a herd of dogs
chased him into
a woman's bathroom
the afternoon dying
with this poem
a quart of beer
& some coke

how you feel?

A Day with Bo

hey you know where to eat.
what time is it.
the white castle.
we with strange people.
hamburgers & cokes. right near the train.
you all got a car.

we left the apartment. to the cold. a gold falcon. we went
                                    up streets &
avenues. snow spotted the tar. the bridges. the tunnels.
where we going.
it's a drive-in. drive up, show your lights & some chick will come.

look at those red lights. step on it. O we can fly.
you all want to fly. lights went by.
red   blue   yellow.
like a merry-go-round,   out of manhattan   into the bronx.
the white castle, like a drive-in movie.
tight-dressed ladies, young & old.
who's going to order.
what you all want.
four hamburgers apiece—
that's sixteen—& four cokes.
ah
are they good hamburgers
naw; fucking horsemeat. they're eighteen cents apiece.
man that's probably cat hive.
shitty bronx cats slain in the back.

the waiter brings the hamburgers, four on a plate.

they wet, man.
some nasty cats.
damn rubber.
how's the coke.
what you want for eighteen cents, people come here from all over the
city cause it's cheap.
look, look at that motherfucker—he got ohio plates. people come
                                        from anywhere
for this bargain.

the car went back thru the streets.
the bronx left where it has always been.
into manhattan.
bellies full of what we wanted—
burgers & cokes.

& eyes that want to get home & fall asleep.

Megalopolis

> (megalopolis—is urban sprawl—as from
> Boston to N.Y.C., Philly, Washington,
> D.C., the cities run into each other)

highway of blood/volkswagens crushed up
against trees
it's a nice highway, ain't it, man
colorful/it'll take you there
will get there round eight with corns on
your ass   from sitting
turn the radio on & listen/   no
turn the shit off
let those lights & trees & rocks
talk/ going by / go by   just sit
back/ we / we go into towns/   sailing the
east coast / westside drive   far-off
buildings look like castles / the kind
dracula flies out of / new england of houses
& fresh butter / you are leaving the nice
section now   no more woods / into rundown
overpopulated areas, low income/ concrete walls
of america / a poet trying to start riots /
arrested with bombs in pockets / conspiracy
to destroy america/ america / united states /
such a simple thing/ lawrence welk- reader's
digest ladies news big hair styles with all
that spray to hold it/ billboards of the highway are singing lies / & as we sail we understand things better / the night of the buildings
we overhead flying by/ singing magic words
of our ancestors.

the Boston roller coaster

1
so boston was like that/the train took its time
cold
& the clouds pissed up the windows
king kong heads went to the last car/   to do
an american thing/ & six times they peed out
the poison / sailors walk with their eyes out
on the ground/ young tight girls going to their
paradise.

2
into provincetown
out of it
new haven
men with wall street in their brief cases
boys sitting together / dazing at the lights
turning / fast / amazement/ their lips almost
kiss.

& soon we'll be in boston.

for dinner / four-day-old chicken sandwich
sold for seventy-five cents / frozen candy
bars / & the man gots to get out before the
wheels turn.

& soon we'll be in boston.

3
it seems like we crossed the atlantic.
we found boston wet/& we found small streets

full of cracks/& we found puddles of water/
& water coming down/ & we found the roller
coaster/ we flew to harvard square.

4
it had good places to grit
rocks by the water/ waves smashing them

at harvard bullshit artists stare at
you from the walls/ outside of boston
small towns with banks you could rob/
high ceilings
where americans eat
& this is such good chicken
& O these rolls are fantastic   they said
a dead roach could be in the coffee.

we sat on a persian rug
we ticked our brains out
tic   tick   ta   tic tick tick tick.

5
windy stairs & parking lots & white stone
are the boston airport
& we went over what we left/ way in the
sky/ the lights of towns / making words
for me
a new york airpoet.

Snaps

monday night
the
winters
grow colder
colder than this

just the projects
on fridays
so good
sometimes the moon
so clear
head to the river
soft noise
of moving water
a ship passing
tugboats
so near
the bright lights
talking to us
in red & blue.

The Group

all thru last
year they sang
& nothing happened
cept the ceiling
almost fell down
one day
& water came down
by the stairs
& the cops came &
took the grass.

so chup chup
bu ra
singing was going
to be life
& they could have
taken planes
all over
& ate lemons when
they got rusty

instead
they went to
jail.

ADVICE TO A PAINTER

them oldies say it was fear
that drove you away
that you sang a song to the
air   & it fell apart

in time going off
soul lights going off
in time
the paintings speaking to you
the river   making you dance

to the
moon
with plans
to leave
for jupiter
in a week
& then to
the stars

in time
winter cold
in time
they move seasons

them oldies
say it was fear

why don't you
go back
& kiss her
in her fat
stomach.

under me sometime. under me. walls & paint. 1967.

when Jade came
he felt the pressure
        &
i did fist strokes
toward him
he said:
where i is, man,
i said:
you uptown, son,
feeling the breeze
he opened his eyes
& he said:
under me something
how do i stop this,
stop what, motherfucker
the walls
colorful paints
things
big-breasted monkies
white priests
with pumpkin-faces
talking books
a pissing t.v. set
strangers walking naked
flying in the air
a kissing horse
a boat coming from that building
        &
where am i anyway,
he said,
with eyes coming out

hey   hey
take it easy, i said
you're here in my house
i'm vic, man

i told you
it was strong
stuff.

Ruskie's Boy

where there was some hole
to show where you was
in those travel dreams
no more corner
no more stoops
                    for you
now the children in the street
play/
ah, but that boy is yours
& your wife dreams on the mattress/
        tell him how we were
nights you come slowly to his room
and stare

and wonder the simple thoughts
the schemes/
                what goes there
so small in the world/
sometime he'll come on top/
&
you will say:
that there is my kid.

Slick

i will have
you meet
my friend
Slick
got his name
three years ago
for being
just that
but
he won't be
the best of
talkers
    unless you
    dig him at
    the bar
    where he is
    the man
    the king
    of take
    them home
whenever there
is a slight
feel of failing
in myself
mentally
he's the man
to look up
or
when my pockets
no longer sing
with coins

he is the best bet
Slick
is the man
into everything
heard of a new place
Slick started it
or he was there
Slick who still
wears bebop hats
Slick who won't
smoke without
Bambu
Slick will one
day write a novel
& Slick will
one day be
the King
of the Annex.

The Eye
Uptown & Downtown
(three days)

1
good things always happen
for instance
cats jump from building
to building in silence.
2
the dope on the
corner moves slowly
junkies dance the
boogaloo.
3
sleeper's head
is crushed against
the concrete
blood stains his ears.
4
one dice weighs
more than the other
knifes went thru space.
5
who knew
who stole
their bullshit
from their lips.
6
the long line
turns
slowly moves
inside.

7
buildings talk spanish
at night.
8
she had everything
she hated.
9
people walk the wall
they let them walk
the water
do the concrete pull.
10
his things are
wherever he wants them
to be
into any street
full.
11
the soft summer wind
has the smell of the
building on the corner.
12
junkies rob their mothers.
13
CURA CURA CURA
BAILA BOOGALOO.
14
watch the clothes burn
& wonder who put it on fire.
15
let the sun
send all it
wants
& we love it.

16
the piano lost its
teeth
the trombone fell apart
the conga drifted.
17
madison is good way
downtown
& way uptown
fuck the middle.
18
the lexington train
broke down.
19
a parade
of smokes
didn't get far.
20
everyone falls asleep
the radio plays memories
glass falls to the floor
the window left open
the lights make shapes
the rooftops hold hands.
21
trees get in the way
of dumb ladies sticking
out of windows.
22
everyday you turn
& turn again
it gets brighter
peep-peep-peep.

23
the stairs are full of holes
one big hole
no stairs.
24
stop sending the
wire downtown
stop talking
& do the rough ride.
25
BANG BANG.
26
small talk
turns into
gutter stomp.
27
the garbage truck
rolled over his ears.
28
what time is the
lame session over.
29
hospitals full with death
pigs
& lonely nurses.
30
death everywhere
coat cut
throat slit
smash against a wall
blood
wallet three feet away
empty.

31
the stories came
this happened
in this manner
which ever
ways.
32
slow the city up
watch
let it all hang out.

WALKING ON THE LIPS OF THE BRONX

1

the frightened bartender hit their heads on the south bronx
police of pipes & cans   iron strings
rides the south bronx   cars full of beer & mafia &
mafia loves   the bridge   under the bridge   by the water
J&B   & the Daily News   news of death   cars broken on the
highway
the man he walked up by the store   in his hands/ he had
a big wall   the big walls   he knew   he knew
who would teach him anything   anything
you got to teach
teach me the ways   O teach me the ways   but what can
you, teacher,
teach the man with the walls/ drop the wall on the corner
by the police   O   yeah   what can you teach the man with the
wall
look at him/walk & talk   look at him / he snagged the wall
out   what can you do
what can you do
talk about a wall/stare at a wall   the man he took the wall
down & threw it against the cars
the big red lips of the south bronx/ right over the water
mr. machine got his head kicked/by the man with the wall
in his hands.

2

open his hands/what he will give you.
brooke avenue could be another thing
or willis   what you find   everything
happens   or what will / walking away
stores in the walls/ talk / something

is happening/the man's eyes were deep
& had ways / to the train & go like
water
kissing the big red lips of the south bronx.

urban dream

1

there was fire & the people were yelling.   running crazing.
screaming & falling.   moving up side down.   there was fire.
fires.   & more fires.   & walls caving to the ground.   & mercy
mercy.   death.   bodies falling down.   under bottles flying in the
air.   garbage cans going up against windows.   a car singing
brightly a blue flame.   a snacth.   a snag.   sounds of bombs.   &
other things blowing up.
times square
electrified.   burned.   smashed. stomped
hey over here
hey you.   where you going.
no walking.   no running.   no standing.
STOP
you crazy.   running.   stick
this stick up your eyes.   pull your heart out.
hey.

2

after noise.   comes silence.   after brightness (or great big flames)
comes darkness.   goes with whispering.   (even soft music can be heard)
even lips smacking.   foots stepping all over bones & ashes, all over
blood & broken lips that left their head somewhere else, all over
livers, & bright white skulls with hair on them. standing over a river
watching hamburgers floating by.   steak with teeth in them.
flags.   & chairs.   & beds.   & golf sets.   & mickey mouse broken in
half.
governors & mayors step out the show.   'they split.

3
dancing arrives.

like in planes.   like in cars.

yes.   yes.   yeah.   mucho boogaloo.   mucho.

& sections of land sail away.   & suicide rises. idiots jumping
into fires.   the brothers five sing the blues as they sink.
kids blow their brains out, first take glue, & then shoot their
skull caps off, with elephant guns.

& someone sings & someone laughes.   & nobody knows.
& chant to gods.
& chant to gods.

spirits

half of his
body hung in
the air
they said it was
magic   a secret
between me & the man
it was no magic that was
in the air   it was no trick
an old lady an old   old lady who
saw the windows open   the wind raising the
curtains   footsteps in an empty room
a young man who saw a t.v. go flying into the
air   a dying lady got up & walked & sang
sudden loss of weight   sudden accident   a car
rolling over a head   a building falling
bad luck   magic.

go after them as they get lost to turn the corner & snag
one   flowers   odors   candles   light candles   morning
noise   papers flying.

a hand thru a wall
is no joke   a mind
going mad at a days
time   so wide
so wide spread
an escape
who escapes   who
runs   run where
from what from
who   a silence
the clouds over

the buildings the
odor in the halls
no one runs
no place to run
no place to hide
traveling   a fast
traveler   a signal
a place   the strange
way the walls start
to act   you say
you say you saw
nothing moving there
you deny a head
a head hiding   behind
the curtains   take
another look
a storm reported
only on your street
someone with grade A
health found dead of
a strange disease
a bad cold
a box found
full of nails
& flowers
names & statues
water sitting under
the beds   blood
falling out of pictures
a flower   burning under
the bed
a lady dressed in
white   flying away

from the roof
waving her hands
for you to follow
you have a bad cold

there is no medicine
there is no cure
there is only a fear
a hope   a waiting
till the spirits
come to our rescue
to your funerals

all the third world
sees spirits &
they talk to them
they are our friends.

DESCARGA

is hanging

over factories
over buildings
say dr. feelgood   what's good
what feels good
aretha comes in   thru big books
over the bridge & into the bronx
is hanging
hanging
yayo el indio
kissing the mike
stealing the oxygen

hanging

ah beep beep
hang   ah beep beep
hanging

bobby ripping bass strings
blood
on the floor

kako
brak   ta ta
bru ta ta
did loco   hanging
over the river
over the river
shhhhhhhhit
over the river

o la la que viene
o la la que viene

kako coming out
of beer bottles
hold up
out over   hanging
over the city
over macys
over steaks
break in kako
steaks get stuck in throats
wine falls over
chombo fingers go to town
brass glows like light
movements like lightning
chombo flying over head
like preaching
smiling & sweating & dancing

hanging

charlie at the door
come in
hang   those keys

break the mirror
break the stones
break the stage
break the waiters
in half
rip
down the curtains
they are bad colors

break the sidewalk

look
is hanging

right over the city
shhhhhhhhhhhhit
let it all hang out

beep ba ba ba
beep ba ba ba

ears bleeding
the nice middle of
the city

blow
blow
&
bang
bang
till people start
jumping into the river.

/ MOVING /

mambo con conga
is Mozambique/

                          for Eddie Palmieri

la caliente   or how would we all
                               talk   if lips are
                               left to us   after
                               an hour or even a minute
                               after

mozab-mozab
                    after a second
                                        he fell back
                                        covered with sweat
                                        leaning
                                        leaning   to a kind
                                        of time   to a
                                        splashes   & we
                                        don't know   not yet

of all those new bags
unopen bags
                    que suene la conga ahora
                    que suene la conga ahora

mam
mam
        we don't know
                    not yet

of all   all those   waves
we fell the nerve   the nerves

127

all of them   but we don't know
yet
     till some-some
                thing
                    comes   running   out
                                                  out
under lights   all   ways
under all the lights
all ways   to sweating
off   off to a start
                         on any
                                 talkers

any   trying to
                      run
& it follows   screams
brings   takes
furious   & destroying/
                         finish   right

fin-
     (& arawaks fly thru the air
       to protect   being   the only
       to save   watch out stepping
                                        now

watch out   softness   to the lights
like forever   could   this   air
could last forever/
                      watch   spots
                      shadows up now
                      shadows   to the
                      floor   outside

                        is   falling   with
                        beats   flying   stepping
        & arawaks like bebops)
                        in stone
                                stoned

how would you talk/sound/dance
in stone

a comer
a comer
            todos a comer
            para   que
            para
            para que
            todas las veces

                        comar
te lo   & forever   some
                                thing

tho   we know not yet
not yet
        shadows   left behind
& mozab   mozab   mozambique
                                thru the veins
                                & mozambique
                                thru the veins
to the heart   the heart/&

                                after
after   in the world
                        cold
fearful   & dry & wet
                        on the earth

all ways
    of
      the ways
ah   ah   the way
thru space
        not sure

a la la la la la
  con tega   lalala
         con te ga   lala
si echo pa'lante
que suene
     (& arawaks be bebops
     bops the arawaks
     bebopping   arawaks
     be bebops)

& he leaned
to the lights
& sweat
     & magic
tho   we understand
        it came
          wondering

dancing up & down the walls
up & down the walls
like suave people
real suave dancer/people
mam———MAM***
mam   mom
     a sky without the blue
     or blackness   a sky

only a sky
he stood   arms in the
air   in front
forever
    & we don't know
    & we don't know

    yet

be the drums/drumming your own death
be they/drumming your own death

mozambique   forever   ever
mozambique/
    listen
    moving   standing
     standing   unfinish
    a new wave

    for ever
    moving/ at the Village Gate/victor

RITMO 1

everybody passed the drummer/ drummers in the park
drummers in the sky/

>   we went up six flights
>   looking down at garages
>   & stores & listening to
>   drums/all the way from
>   the park/all the way from
>   the sky

everybody
staring out/riding the roofs/ look at the lights
of palisades/ the round circles in the black sky
float all the way to the edge of the park/standing
by the river   the blue lights & red lights of
commerce/the windows of brooklyn/

>   monk dropped his glass
>   on someone's head/cause
>   that's what he wanted to
>   do/all over a shirt/& what
>   about it

everybody
hanging on like clothes on the line/ drummers
writing poems in the sky/drummers   pulling off
their shirts/the trees echo the passages/ & we on
the roof quietly resting/ looking at summer/ at
the lights that the city creates/the airplanes
shoot by   over highways   & rivers/

everybody
passed by the drummers/ roofs & windows over
head & eyes on fire

ALONE/december/night

it's been so long
speaking to people
who think it all
too complex
stupidity in their eyes
&
it's been so long
so far from the truth
so far from a roof
to talk to
or a hand to touch
or anything to really
love

it's been so long
talking to myself
alone
in the night
listening to a music
that is me.

Victor Cruz was born in Aguas Buenas, Puerto Rico, in 1949. His family moved to New York City in 1954. Mr. Cruz attended Benjamin Franklin High School and is now associated with the Gut Theater on East 104th Street.

His poems have appeared in Evergreen Review, New York Review of Books, Ramparts, Umbra, of which he was an editor, Down Here, and several small magazines, and have also been included in two recently published anthologies.